Our Favorite JAMAICAN RECIPES

THREE JAMAICAN DAUGHTERS REMEMBER THEIR MOTHERS' COOKING

Trudy Hanks nee Pilliner
Maureen Tapper nee Pilliner
Rebecca Marshall nee Tapper

ACKNOWLEDGMENTS

We could not have done it without our photographers, tasters, and contributors:

Don Hanks

Gordon Tapper

Trevor Marshall

Teddy & Rosy Pilliner

Margaret Marshall

COPYRIGHT, LEGAL NOTICE & DISCLAIMERS

FOREWORD

This book is dedicated to our Mothers:
Enid Pilliner and Enid Tapper

Once upon a time (in the late 1960's), a Boy met a Girl and it became obvious that his family and her family were destined to be together – the Boy was an only son and had the same first name as the Girl's brother, who was also an only son; both mothers had the same first name; and the Boy's father had the same nickname as the Girl's brother.

The Boy and the Girl decided that fate and love were on their side and they married in 1972. Both families, and extended members, have been living happily in harmony ever since.

The mothers of both families were totally dedicated to their family, and food was just one of the many ways that they showed how important their families were to them. These recipes do not just represent food, but happy memories of love and a childhood, long gone, but fondly remembered.

We are not professional cooks. We have tested these recipes* that were cooked by our mothers when we were growing up in Jamaica, and we continue to enjoy these meals in our homes today – we hope you will enjoy them, too.

> Trudy Hanks nee Pilliner
> Maureen Tapper nee Pilliner
> Rebecca Marshall nee Tapper

Our Favorite JAMAICAN RECIPES is also available as an E-Book.

Visit our website and Facebook page:
www.OurFavoriteJamaicanRecipes.com
www.Facebook.com/OurFavoriteJamaicanRecipes.com

*All recipe photographs are actual results of the recipes in this book.

TABLE OF CONTENTS

Crayfish (Janga) Soup

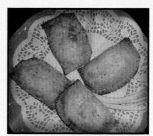

Beef Patty

Curry Chicken

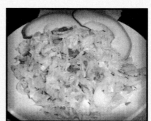

Salt Fish and Cabbage

TABLE OF CONTENTS

Corn Pudding

Cinnamon Buns

Ice Box Cake

Rock Cakes

TABLE OF CONTENTS

Rum Punch

Ackee

Breadfruit

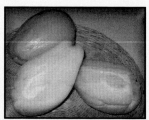

Cho Cho

Scotch Bonnet Pepper

SOUPS

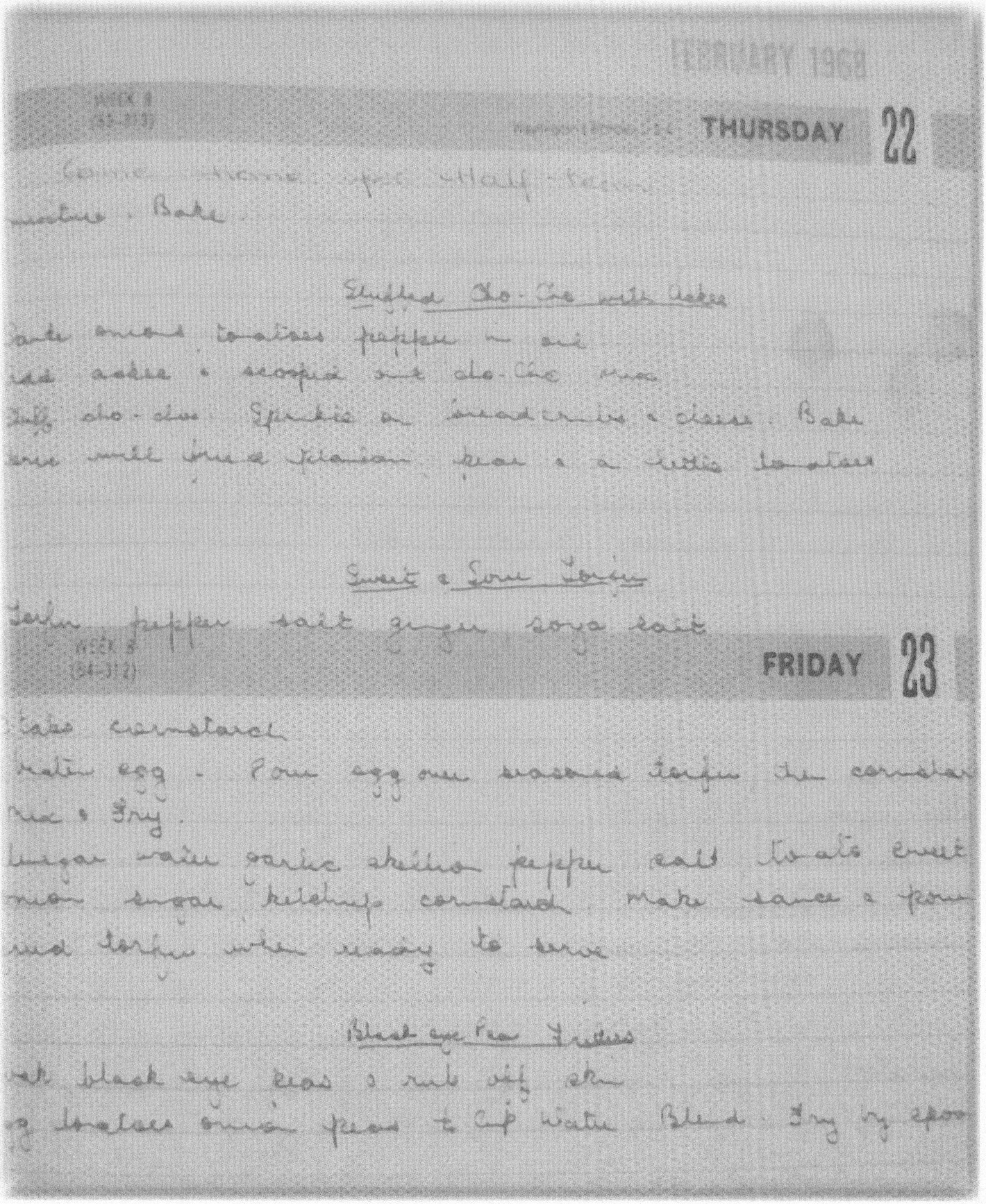

THURSDAY 22

Come home for Half-term

Stuffed Cho-Cho with Ackee

Sweet & Sour Tofu

FRIDAY 23

Black eye Pea Fritters

Copy of Recipes handwritten by Enid Pilliner (1969)
No paper surface was safe, when Mother needed to write down recipes.

BEEF SOUP

*Saturday is Soup Day
in most Jamaican homes.*

BEEF SOUP

16 cups water
2   pounds beef, cubed
6   teaspoons beef instant bouillon
2   cups pumpkin*, peeled and cubed
1   stalk scallion, chopped
1   medium onion, chopped
1   small turnip, peeled and cubed
2   sprigs fresh thyme

2   medium carrots, peeled and cubed
1   large cho cho (chayote squash), peeled and cubed
2   medium white potatoes, peeled and cubed
½   pound yellow yam (namé), peeled and cubed
1   scotch bonnet pepper, whole
1   cup all-purpose flour (for dumplings**)
½   cup water
    Salt to taste

1. To boiling water – add beef, instant bouillon, 1 cup pumpkin cubes, scallion, onion, thyme, and turnip.
2. Cook until beef is tender.
3. Mash cooked pumpkin against inside of pot to give soup a yellow color.
4. Add the remaining pumpkin cubes, carrot, cho cho, white potato, yellow yam, scotch bonnet pepper, and dumplings**.
5. Add salt to taste and more water for desired consistency.
6. Simmer for about 30 minutes, or until vegetables are cooked and soup thickens.
7. If you like a spicy soup, mash the scotch bonnet pepper against the inside of the pot, and stir gently making sure that no seeds get into the soup***.
8. Remove scotch bonnet pepper.
Makes 4 to 6 servings.

* West Indian Pumpkin, see NOTES: Pumpkin - Page 73.
**To make dumplings, see NOTES: Dumplings for Stew and Soups - Page 72.
***See NOTES: Scotch Bonnet Pepper - Page 74.

CRAYFISH (JANGA) SOUP

Trips from our home in the parish of St. Ann to visit grandparents, aunts, and uncles in the parish of Westmoreland, were always exciting. We always left home by 4:00 a.m. for the three-hour trip. Once in the car, the three children would promptly fall asleep, but would awake, without prompting, for the last hour of the journey to lustily sing the Fats Domino songs, "Hello Josephine" and "Blueberry Hill", again, and again...

There were four homes to visit, with a meal at each one. We always visited our paternal grandparents first, just in time for breakfast with the best chocolate tea ever; plus whatever else was being served. But, the most anticipated meal was Aunt Vie's Janga Soup made from the crayfish caught in the river that ran through her property.

It was then time to make the return trip, to sleep in the car until we would be awakened at home by our ever vigilant Mother who was the best driver who never ever drove a car, and who never slept whilst Dad was driving.

A Pilliner Family Memory

CRAYFISH (JANGA*) SOUP

1	pound uncooked whole crayfish**	6	small okras
½	chicken breast	1	small onion, diced
12	cups water	2	stalks scallion, chopped
1	pound yellow yam (namé), optional	2	cloves garlic, minced
1	medium white potato, cubed	3	sprigs fresh thyme or ½ teaspoon dry thyme
1	cho cho (chayote squash), cubed	1	scotch bonnet pepper, whole
2	green bananas, cut in 1 inch pieces		Salt and ground black pepper to taste
1	small turnip, cubed	1	cup all-purpose flour (for dumplings***)
1	medium carrot, cubed		

1. Rinse shrimp** and set aside.
2. Bring water to a boil in a large stock pot.
3. Add chicken breast, scallion, and a pinch of salt. Boil for 15 minutes.
4. Remove chicken breast, cool, shred and return to pot.
5. Add all ingredients, except flour, and boil for 15 minutes .
6. Make dumplings*** and add to pot. Simmer for 15 minutes.
7. Add shrimp**. Stir and simmer for 10 minutes.

Serve hot.

Makes 4 to 6 servings.

* Janga (crayfish) is the name given to fresh-water shrimp found in many Jamaican rivers. These crayfish are not like the crayfish/crawfish/crawdad that have a hard shell and are more like a small lobster.

**Fresh, large, sea-water shrimp with heads on, were used in this recipe in the place of crayfish.

*** To make dumplings, see NOTES: Dumplings for Stew and Soups - Page 72.

PEPPER POT SOUP

For obvious reasons, a family member who was not born in Jamaica, called this Green Soup. He loved it, but we were never able to convince him to eat the pig's tail.

A Pilliner Family Memory

PEPPER POT SOUP

1 pound salted beef (corned beef), cubed	2 teaspoons onion powder
1 pound salted pig's tail (traditional, but optional), cut in 2-inch pieces	
14 cups water	2 medium sweet potatoes, peeled and cubed
1 medium onion, chopped	2 medium white potatoes, peeled and cubed
2 stalks scallion, chopped	¼ pound yellow yam (namé), peeled and cubed
3 sprigs fresh thyme	1 scotch bonnet pepper, whole
2 cloves garlic, chopped	1 cup all-purpose flour (for dumplings**)
1 (15 ounce can) callaloo* (Jamaican Spinach)	Salt to taste
½ teaspoon ground black pepper	

1. Boil salted meat (beef and pig's tail) in water for 20 minutes. Discard water and repeat this step.
2. In large pot, add 14 cups of water to the salted meat, and half of the onion, scallion, thyme, and garlic.
3. Boil for 1½ hours or pressure-cook*** for 30 to 35 minutes, until meat is tender.
4. Chop callaloo in food processor and add to pot with meat.
5. Add black pepper, onion powder, white and sweet potatoes, yellow yam, dumplings**, whole scotch bonnet pepper and remaining onion, scallion, thyme, and garlic. Salt to taste.
6. Add more water for desired consistency
7. Simmer for 35 to 40 minutes, or until potatoes and yam are cooked.

Makes 4 to 6 servings.

*The authentic ingredient is Indian Kale which is not easily available. Spinach may be substituted.
**To make dumplings, see NOTES: Dumplings for Stew and Soups - Page 72.
***Follow manufacturer's instructions.

RED PEAS SOUP

RED PEAS SOUP

½	pound salted beef (corned beef), cubed	3	teaspoons dried thyme
½	pound salted pig's tail, cut in 2-inch pieces	1	scotch bonnet pepper, whole
8	cups water	½	cup coconut milk
2	cups dry red kidney beans*, soaked in water overnight		
½	pound fresh beef, cubed	6	pimento (allspice) seeds
½	teaspoon ground black pepper	2	medium carrots, cubed
1	medium onion, chopped	2	medium white potatoes, cubed
2	stalks scallions, chopped	1	cup all-purpose flour (for dumplings**)
2	cloves garlic, minced		Salt to taste

1. Boil pig's tails and salted beef in water in a large pot for 20 minutes. Discard water and repeat this step.
2. Add 8 cups of water, kidney beans, fresh beef, black pepper, onion, scallion, garlic, and thyme to pot with boiled salted meat.
3. Cook for about 1 hour or until meat and kidney beans are tender.
4. Add whole scotch bonnet pepper, coconut milk, pimento seeds, carrots, potatoes, and dumplings**. Season to taste.
5. Simmer for an additional 30 minutes.
6. Remove scotch bonnet pepper and pimento seeds (if possible).

Makes 4 to 6 servings.

*Canned red kidney beans may be used and will not need to be soaked, but final product will not have the traditional, dark red color that dry beans produce.

**To make dumplings, see NOTES: Dumplings for Stew and Soups - Page 72.

ENTREES

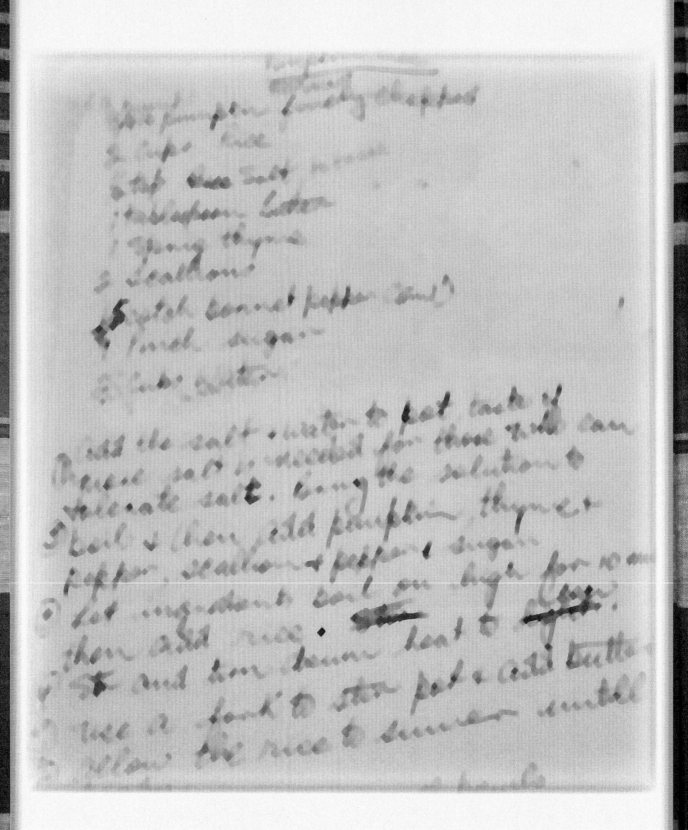

ACKEE
and SALT FISH

This is the National Dish of Jamaica.

Usually eaten for breakfast, but is also enjoyed for lunch or dinner.

ACKEE and SALT* FISH

½ pound boneless salted fish (cod or pollock)
2 slices bacon, minced (optional)
1 tablespoon vegetable or coconut oil
2 stalks scallion, chopped
1 medium onion, chopped
1 small tomato, chopped
½ scotch bonnet pepper, chopped (no seeds)
1 (19 ounce) can ackee in brine, drained
1 teaspoon black pepper

1. Soak salted fish in cold water for about 1 hour. Discard water.
2. Add salted fish to fresh water. Boil for 15 minutes.
3. Discard water and flake salted fish. Set aside.
4. Heat vegetable oil or fry bacon pieces (for grease and flavor) until crisp.
5. Add onion, scallion, tomato, and scotch bonnet pepper. Saute.
6. Add flaked salted fish, ackee, and black pepper. Stir lightly.
7. Cover and simmer for about 5 minutes.

Makes 4 to 6 servings.

Serve with boiled green bananas, boiled or fried** dumplings, bammy***, or boiled yellow yam (namé)***.

*See NOTES: Salt Fish - Page 73.
**Recipe is included in this book - Page 37.
*** See NOTES: Bammy and Yellow Yam - Pages 71 and 74.

BEEF PATTY

This is a very popular Jamaican food. Patties are available in most corner stores and are rarely cooked at home. But, that didn't stop Mother – she was even known to fry, instead of bake, patties!

Our favorite Patty memories were made on Friday evenings when we would visit the soda fountain at Coronation Drugstore in Claremont. We would sit on the swiveling stools, eat patties that had more flour than meat filling, and savor the taste of malted milk that was so delicious – we have never found its equal.

A Pilliner Family Memory

BEEF PATTY

PASTRY
2	cups all-purpose flour	¼	cup margarine
¼	teaspoon salt	⅓	cup cold water
½	teaspoon Jamaican curry powder		

1. Sift all-purpose flour, curry powder, and salt into a large bowl.
2. Cut in the margarine until crumbly.
3. Add cold water to make a stiff dough.
4. Lightly flour a smooth surface and roll out dough until about ⅛ inch thick. Cut in 6-inch circles.
5. Cover with wax paper or damp cloth until ready to use. Dough can be placed in refrigerator overnight. If you do refrigerate, remove the dough at least 15 minutes before using.

MEAT FILLING
2	tablespoons vegetable oil	½	teaspoon curry powder
1	small onion, finely chopped	½	teaspoon dried thyme
¼	teaspoon scotch bonnet pepper, chopped (no seeds)		
1	pound lean ground beef	¼	cup breadcrumbs
½	teaspoon salt	¼	cup breadcrumbs
½	teaspoon ground black pepper		

Heat oven to 375° F.
1. In heavy skillet, heat the vegetable oil and saute the onion and scotch bonnet pepper until soft.
2. Add the ground beef, salt, pepper, curry powder, and thyme.
3. Cook for about 10 minutes, or until meat is browned.
4. Add breadcrumbs and stock. Combine all ingredients well.
5. Cover the skillet and simmer for about 10 to 15 minutes, stirring occasionally.
6. When liquid has been absorbed, the filling is ready. It should be moist, but not watery.
7. Remove skillet from flame and allow meat mixture to cool.
8. Uncover the dough circles and place 2 to 3 tablespoons of meat filling on half of each circle.
9. Moisten the edges of the dough with water and fold the dough circle over the meat filling.
10. Pinch the edges closed with a fork.
11. Lightly brush the pastry with a mixture of 1 egg beaten with 1 teaspoon water.
12. Bake on a lightly greased baking sheet for 30 to 40 minutes, or until golden brown.
Makes 10 to 12 Beef Patties.

BEEF ROAST

When we were growing up in Jamaica, rare or medium roast beef, was unheard of. All meats were well cooked and well seasoned from the day before.

BEEF ROAST

3   pounds beef bottom round or chuck roast
1   medium onion, minced
2   stalks skallion, mashed and minced
2   cloves garlic, minced
2   teaspoons dried thyme
½   scotch bonnet pepper, minced (no seeds)
1   teaspoon vinegar
1   tablespoon garlic powder
1   teaspoon ground black pepper
3   teaspoons instant beef bouillon
½   cup water or beef stock
4   large white potatoes, halved
4   large carrots, cut in half lengthwise

Heat oven to 355ºF.
1. Combine green pepper, onion, skallion, garlic, thyme, and scotch bonnet pepper.
2. Make small incisions in meat and fill with seasoning mixture. Retain unused seasoning mixture for later use.
3. Combine black pepper, garlic powder, and instant beef bouillon.
4. Rub meat with vinegar, then with black pepper mixture.
5. Marinate in refrigerator overnight, or for at least 2 hours.
6. Place meat in large roasting pan and cover with aluminum foil.
7. Cook in oven for 1½ hour.
8. Pour ½ cup water or beef stock into pan along with the seasoning mixture that was left over from stuffing the meat.
9. Add potatoes and carrots. Re-cover roasting pan and cook for about 1 hour or until meat is tender.
Makes 6 to 8 servings.

BEEF STEW

BEEF STEW

2	pounds beef, cubed	3½	cups water
1	medium onion, chopped	¼	cup ketchup
2	stalks scallion, chopped		Salt to taste
2	cloves garlic, minced	2	medium carrots, cut in 2-inch pieces
2	sprigs fresh thyme, chopped	2	small white potatoes, cubed
4	teaspoons instant beef bouillon	1	medium cabbage, cut in wedges
1	teaspoon black pepper	1	cup all-purpose flour (for dumplings*)
1	tablespoon Worcestershire sauce		Cornstarch or flour
2	tablespoons vegetable oil		

1. Season meat with onion, scallion, garlic, thyme, beef bouillon, black pepper, and Worcestershire sauce.
2. Marinate in the refrigerator overnight, or for at least 2 hours.
3. Brown beef in vegetable oil in large saucepan.
4. Add ketchup and water; bring to a boil, then lower heat.
5. Cook on medium heat for about 1 hour, or until meat is tender.
6. Add salt if needed, carrots, potatoes, cabbage, and dumplings*.
7. Cook for 30 minutes, then thicken with cornstarch or flour, if desired.
8. Remove core from cabbage before serving.

Makes 4 to 6 servings.

*To make dumplings, see NOTES: Dumplings for Stew and Soups - Page 72.

CALLALOO
and SALT FISH

Callaloo and Salt Fish is usually eaten at breakfast accompanied by boiled green bananas, roasted breadfruit or fried dumplings.

CALLALOO* and SALT FISH**

½   pound boneless salted fish (cod or pollock)
1   tablespoon vegetable oil
1   medium onion, chopped
2   stalks scallion, chopped
2   sprigs fresh thyme, chopped
½   scotch bonnet pepper, chopped (no seeds)
½   teaspoon black pepper
½   teaspoon vinegar
4   cups fresh callaloo* *(including stalks), chopped and rinsed
1   medium tomato, chopped
    Salt to taste

1. Boil salted fish for 15 minutes or until tender. Discard water and flake salted fish. Set aside.
2. Heat oil in frying pan and saute onion, scallion, thyme, and scotch bonnet pepper for 5 minutes.
3. Add callaloo**, vinegar, and water. Cover pan and steam on low heat for 15 minutes.
4. Add flaked salted fish and tomato. Add salt to taste.
5. Steam for 10 minutes.

*See NOTES: Callaloo - Page 71. If canned callaloo is used, it is not necessary to cook it for 15 minutes. Add callaloo and vinegar (no water), at the same time as salted fish and tomatoes.
**See NOTES: Salt Fish - Page 73.

COOK-UP RICE
with BULLY BEEF
and CABBAGE

Canned Corned Beef is referred to as Bully Beef in the United Kingdom. It was issued as rations to soldiers in the British Army from the late 1800's until recent years.

Bully Beef is widely used in Jamaica. Straight out of the can to make sandwiches, or cooked and served for breakfast, lunch, or dinner.

COOK-UP RICE with BULLY BEEF and CABBAGE

2   tablespoons vegetable oil
1   large onion, chopped
2   cloves garlic, minced
2   stalks scallion, chopped
½   scotch bonnet pepper, chopped (no seeds)
1   teaspoon ground black pepper
1   teaspoon dried thyme
1   large carrot, chopped
1   small green sweet pepper, diced
3   cups cabbage, chopped
1   (12 ounce) can bully beef* (corned beef)
4   cups hot water
2   teaspoons instant chicken bouillon
     Salt to taste
2   cups rice, uncooked

1. Heat oil in a 4-quart pot and saute chopped onion, garlic, scallion, scotch bonnet pepper, black pepper, and thyme.
2. Add carrot, green pepper, and cabbage.
3. Stir in bully beef *(corned beef).
4. Add hot water and instant bouillon cubes. Salt to taste.
5. Add rice, mix well and lower flame.
6. Cook covered for about 30 minutes or until rice grains are soft and water absorbed.
Serve hot.
Makes 4 to 6 servings.

*1 pound ground beef may be substituted for the bully beef (corned beef). Ground beef should be browned, before adding it to the pot.

COOK-UP RICE with PUMPKIN and SALT FISH

COOK-UP RICE with PUMPKIN* and SALT FISH**

½   pound boneless salted fish (cod or pollock)
3½ cups water
2½ cups pumpkin*, peeled and diced
     Pinch of sugar
2   tablespoons margarine
1   sprig fresh thyme, chopped
2   scallions, chopped
1   small onion, chopped
½   scotch bonnet pepper, chopped (no seeds)
1   cup cabbage, chopped
2   cups long grain rice
     Salt and ground black pepper to taste

1. Boil salted fish for 15 minutes. Discard water.
2. Cut salted fish into small cubes and set aside.
3. In 2-quart pot, bring 3½ cups water to a boil.
4. Add pumpkin cubes and sugar. Boil on high heat for 10 minutes.
5. Heat margarine in a frying pan and saute thyme, scallion, onion, scotch bonnet pepper, cabbage, and salted fish.
6. Add fish mixture to pot with pumpkin.
7. Add rice. Salt and black pepper to taste.
8. Mash some of the pumpkin cubes to ensure a nice pumpkin color when rice is cooked.
9. Stir to mix all ingredients.
10. Lower heat and simmer for about 30 minutes, or until rice is cooked and liquid absorbed.
Makes 4 to 6 servings.

* West Indian Pumpkin. See Notes: Pumpkin - Page 73.
**See NOTES: Salt Fish - Page 73.

CURRY
CHICKEN

CURRY CHICKEN

1	whole chicken, cut in small pieces
6	tablespoons Jamaican curry powder
3	teaspoons instant chicken bouillon
2	teaspoons ground black pepper
1	medium onion, chopped
2	stalks scallion, chopped
3	sprigs fresh thyme, chopped
3	cloves garlic, chopped
1	scotch bonnet pepper, chopped (no seeds)
	Vegetable oil for frying
2	medium white potatoes, cubed
3	cups water
	Salt to taste
	Cornstarch, if needed

1. Season chicken with all ingredients except oil, potatoes, and water.
2. Marinate in the refrigerator overnight, or for at least 2 hours.
3. Heat oil in large sauce pan and add chicken. Cook for 5 to 10 minutes, stirring continuously so that chicken does not burn.
4. Add water and cook over medium heat for about 30 minutes, then add potato cubes. Salt to taste.
5. Cook for an additional 20 minutes or until chicken is fully cooked.
6. Thicken with cornstarch, if needed.

Serve with Rice and Peas*, and Cabbage, Carrot and Tomato Salad*.

Makes 4 to 6 servings.

*Recipes are included in this book - Pages 34 and 39.

CURRY GOAT

No large gathering, whether it be a wedding, funeral, or party, is complete unless Curry Goat is served.

"Mannish Water", which is a very spicy soup made from the goat's head and tripe, and vegetables, is also served before the main meal.

CURRY GOAT

3 pounds goat meat*(with bones), cut in medium-sized pieces

6 tablespoons Jamaican curry powder
5 teaspoons instant beef bouillon
2 teaspoons ground black pepper
2 medium onions, chopped
2 stalks scallion, chopped
3 sprigs fresh thyme, chopped
4 cloves garlic, minced
1 scotch bonnet pepper, chopped (no seeds)

Vegetable oil for frying
2 medium white potatoes, cubed
2 medium carrots, cubed (optional)
Water
Salt to taste
Cornstarch or flour, as needed

1. Season meat with curry powder, beef bouillon, black pepper, onion, scallion, scotch bonnet pepper, garlic, and thyme.
2. Marinate in the refrigerator overnight, or for at least 2 hours.
3. Heat oil in large sauce pan and add meat. Cook for 5 to 10 minutes, stirring continuously so that meat does not burn.
4. Add enough water to cover the meat and seasoning.
5. Bring to a boil, then reduce heat and cook for about 1½ hours or until meat is tender.
6. Add potato and carrot. Salt to taste.
7. Simmer for 30 minutes or until potatoes and carrots are tender.
8. Thicken with cornstarch, if desired.

Serve with Rice and Peas**, boiled green bananas or Cabbage, Carrot and Tomato Salad**.
Makes 5 to 6 servings.

*You may use this recipe for lamb or beef.
**Recipes are included in this book - Page 39.

CURRIED (DRIED) SHRIMP

Although Jamaica is an island, fresh shrimp or lobster was not always available if you lived in the interior. We discovered dried shrimp at our neighborhood supermarket which was owned by a Chinese family, and Curried (Dried) Shrimp became a favorite family meal.

A Pilliner Family Memory

CURRIED (DRIED) SHRIMP

1   (3 ounce) package dried shrimp
    Vegetable oil for frying
1   small onion, diced
1   teaspoon Jamaican curry powder
½   cup water or chicken stock
1   cup sweet green peas
    Salt to taste
¼   teaspoon all-purpose flour (optional)

1. Reconstitute dried shrimp by soaking them in water for 1 hour, then discard water.
2. Heat vegetable oil in frying pan on medium heat. Saute diced onions.
3. Add curry powder and cook for 30 seconds.
4. Add shrimp and water or chicken stock. Simmer for 20 minutes.
5. Add sweet green peas and salt to taste. Simmer for an additional 5 minutes.
6. Thicken with all-purpose flour, if desired. Cook for 2 minutes.

Makes 4 to 5 servings.

ESCOVEITCH FISH

This is a very popular Jamaican dish and is cooked using any of the fish supplied by local fishermen: red or yellow snapper; king fish; parrot fish; goat fish; or mullet. Except in hotels and high-end restaurants, you will not find escoveitch fish made with fillets – half of the fun is battling with the bones.

Bammy and roasted breadfruit are delicious accompaniments to Escoveitch Fish.

The word escoveitch is a Jamaican derivative of the Spanish word, escabeche. Escabeche is a dish of fish, chicken or pork that is marinated in an acidic mixture and is very popular in Spain and Latin America.

ESCOVEITCH FISH

3	pounds fish (yellow-tail or red snapper), cut in 3-inch slices*		
1	tablespoon salt	1	large carrot, julienned
1	tablespoon ground black pepper	1	large onion, sliced
¼	cup all-purpose flour	1	scotch bonnet pepper, chopped (no seeds)
	Vegetable oil for frying	½	teaspoon salt
2	cups white vinegar	1	teaspoon pimento (allspice) seeds

1. Rub fish with salt and black pepper.
2. Dust fish with a thin coating of flour.
3. Fry fish on both sides, drain, and place in a deep dish.
4. In medium saucepan, combine vinegar, carrot, onion, scotch bonnet pepper, salt, and pimento (allspice) seeds.
5. Bring to a boil and simmer until onion is tender.
6. Pour vinegar mixture over the fish.
7. Marinate for at least 1 hour before serving. Refrigerate if marinating over 2 hours.

Serve cold or warm.

Makes 4 to 6 servings.

*Traditionally, whole fish is used in this recipe, but fillets may also be used. Flounder fillets are good in this recipe.

This recipe may also be made with chicken legs or thighs.

FRICASSEE CHICKEN

This is also called Brown Stew Chicken.

FRICASSEE CHICKEN
(BROWN STEW CHICKEN)

1   whole chicken, cut up
1   teaspoon instant chicken bouillon
1   teaspoon ground black pepper
2 + 2 tablespoons of soy sauce
1   medium onion, chopped
3   stalks of scallion, chopped
1   scotch bonnet pepper, chopped (no seeds)
1   medium sweet pepper (green or red), chopped
3   cloves garlic, chopped
½   teaspoon fresh grated ginger
2   medium tomatoes, cubed
3   sprigs of fresh thyme, chopped
     Vegetable oil for frying
2   cups water
     All-purpose flour or cornstarch

1. Season chicken with salt, pepper, 2 tablespoons soy sauce, onion, scallion, scotch bonnet pepper, sweet pepper, garlic, ginger, tomato, and thyme.
2. Marinate for at least 1 hour. (Refrigerate if marinating for more than 2 hours.)
3. Remove chicken pieces from seasoning vegetables.
4. In large frying pan, heat vegetable oil. Fry chicken pieces until they are browned on all sides.
5. Remove chicken from pan and drain off most of the vegetable oil.
6. Add seasoning vegetables and saute for 3 minutes.
7. Add water and 2 tablespoons soy sauce. Simmer for 5 minutes.
8. Add chicken and simmer for about 25 minutes or until chicken is fully cooked.
9. Thicken with flour or cornstarch, if desired.
10. Simmer for 5 minutes, stirring occasionally.

Makes 6 to 8 servings.

OXTAIL
and BUTTER BEANS

OXTAIL and BUTTER BEANS

2   pounds oxtail, cut in 2-inch pieces
1   medium onion, chopped
2   stalks scallion, chopped
½   teaspoon scotch bonnet pepper, chopped (no seeds)
2   cloves garlic, minced
3   sprigs of fresh thyme, chopped
½   teaspoon ground allspice
3   teaspoons instant beef bouillon
1   teaspoon ground black pepper
2   teaspoons Worcestershire sauce
   Vegetable oil for frying
2   tomatoes, cubed
1   medium carrot, cubed
6   cups of water
   Salt to taste
2   (15 ounce) cans butter beans

1. Add onion, scallion, scotch bonnet pepper, garlic, thyme, allspice, beef bouillon, black pepper, and Worcestershire sauce to oxtail.
2. Marinate in the refrigerator overnight, or for at least 2 hours.
3. Fry the oxtail and seasoning in vegetable oil for about 10 minutes, or until browned on all sides.
4. Add water, tomato, and carrot. Salt to taste.
5. Simmer for about 1½ hours or until oxtail is tender.
6. Add the beans and simmer for about 20 to 30 minutes

Makes 4 to 6 servings.

TIP: If you have family members who like the taste of oxtail, but do not like the bones, add an additional ½ pound of beef cut in 2-inch cubes to this recipe.

PIG'S
TROTTERS

The only son in the Tapper family was very mischievous and cunning as a boy. He somehow convinced his youngest sister that pig's trotters were not good eating, and that he would "help her" by eating her share.

Sister was happy that he was so nice to her, and it was almost a year before she wised up and noticed how much he enjoyed this food that he claimed was neither delicious, nor good for her. She decided to make the sacrifice and try a piece herself... and that was the day his double portion of pig's trotters ended!

A Tapper Family Memory

PIG'S TROTTERS

3 pounds pig's trotters (feet), cut lengthwise and crosswise
   Water or chicken stock
4 cloves of garlic, chopped
1 large onion, chopped
3 stalks scallions, chopped
2 sprigs of fresh thyme, chopped
1 teaspoon ground black pepper
2 tablespoons ketchup
1 (15 ounce) can of butter beans
   Salt to taste

1. Wash pig's trotters in cold water and vinegar. Discard water.
2. Fill large pot with enough liquid (water or chicken stock) to cover the trotters.
3. Add half of the garlic, onion, scallion, and thyme.
4. Bring to a boil, then lower temperature to maintain a simmer.
5. Simmer for 2 to 3 hours or until trotters are soft and falling off the bones. (May be cooked in a pressure cooker* for 35 to 40 minutes, or in a slow cooker* for 5 hours on high or 6 hours on low.)
6. Add remaining garlic, onion, scallions and thyme, black pepper, ketchup, and butter beans. Salt to taste.
7. Simmer for about ½ hour or until mixture thickens.

*Follow manufacturer's instructions.

PORK ROAST

Together with roasted chicken, this was a Sunday dinner favorite.

It was delicious, and the "crackling" that was formed when the skin crisped, made it even more enjoyable.

A Pilliner Family Memory

PORK ROAST

2	pounds fresh pork leg, with skin on	1	small slice of ginger, minced
1	onion, chopped	2	teaspoons black pepper
3	cloves garlic, minced	2	teaspoons instant chicken bouillon
1	stalk scallion, minced		Vegetable oil for frying
2	sprigs of thyme, minced		Water or chicken stock
½	scotch bonnet pepper, minced (no seeds)		All-purpose flour for gravy

Heat oven to 400ºF.

1. Combine onion, garlic, scallion, thyme, scotch bonnet pepper, ginger, black pepper, and instant bouillon.
2. Make several incisions in the pork leg with a sharp knife and stuff with some of the seasoning mixture*. Rub remaining seasoning mixture over surface of pork leg.
3. Marinate in the refrigerator overnight, or for at least 2 hours.
4. Heat vegetable oil in a large frying pan. Brown meat on all sides.
5. Transfer meat to a roasting pan – skin side up.
6. Add ¼ cup of water or chicken stock to the frying pan and stir. Add this mixture to the roasting pan.
7. Cover and cook in oven for 1 hour**.
8. Remove cover from roasting pan. Score pork skin to produce "crackling". Roast uncovered for 1 hour, or until well cooked.
9. Remove meat from oven and let sit for ½ hour before slicing.
10. To make gravy, add ¼ cup water mixed with ½ teaspoon of flour to the drippings that have formed in roasting pan.

Makes 4 to 6 servings.

*If meat has been boned, rub seasoning on the inside and outside of the pork leg and tie together with twine to make it compact.
**A boned leg will cook faster.

SALT FISH
and CABBAGE

SALT FISH* and CABBAGE

1   pound boneless salted fish (cod or pollock)
    Vegetable oil for frying
1   small cabbage, roughly shredded
1   medium onion, chopped
2   cloves garlic, chopped
2   stalks scallion, chopped
2   sprigs fresh thyme or 1 teaspoon dry thyme
1   small tomato, chopped
½   scotch bonnet pepper, chopped (no seeds)
½   teaspoon ground black pepper
    Salt to taste

1. Wash salted fish and boil in water for 15 minutes, or until tender.
2. Discard water. Flake salted fish.
3. Saute cabbage in vegetable oil with half of the onion and garlic, until cabbage is wilted but still crisp.
    Remove from frying pan.
4. Fry remaining onion and garlic, scallion, thyme, tomato, scotch bonnet pepper, and black pepper
    for 5 minutes.
5. Add flaked salted fish and cook for another 5 minutes.
6. Return cooked cabbage mixture to frying pan. Mix until all ingredients are combined.
7. Add salt to taste.
8. Simmer for 5 minutes to combine flavors.
Makes 4 to 6 servings.

*See NOTES: Salt Fish - Page 73.

STEW
PEAS

STEW PEAS

2 cups dried red kidney beans*, soaked in water overnight

½ pound salted beef (corned beef), cubed	3 sprigs fresh thyme, chopped
½ pound salted pig's tail, cut in 2-inch pieces	1 scotch bonnet pepper, whole
½ pound fresh beef, cubed	8 cups water
½ teaspoon ground black pepper	2 cups coconut milk
1 medium onion, chopped	6 pimento (allspice) seeds
2 stalks scallions, chopped	1 cup all-purpose flour (for dumplings**)
2 cloves garlic, minced	Salt to taste

1. Boil salted meat (pig's tails and salted beef) in a medium pot for about 30 minutes. Discard water and repeat this step.
2. Season fresh beef cubes with black pepper, onion, scallion, garlic, and thyme.
3. Add 8 cups of water, fresh beef with seasoning, and soaked peas to pot with salted meat.
4. Cook for about 1 hour, or until meat and kidney beans are tender.
5. Add whole scotch bonnet pepper, coconut milk, pimento (allspice) seeds, and dumplings**. Add salt to taste.
6. Cook for 30 to 40 minutes.
7. Thicken mixture with 1 tablespoon of flour mixed with ¼ cup of water, if desired.
8. Remove scotch bonnet pepper and pimento (allspice) seeds.

Makes 6 to 8 servings.

*Canned red kidney beans may be used, but the final product will not have the traditional, dark red color that dry beans produce.
** To make dumplings, see NOTES: Dumplings for Stew and Soups - Page 72.

STUFFED CHO CHO*

STUFFED CHO CHO

3   large unpeeled cho cho (chayote squash)
½   teaspoon salt
½   pound ground beef
1   small onion, diced
¼   teaspoon dried thyme
¼   teaspoon scotch bonnet pepper, diced (no seeds)
2   teaspoons instant beef bouillon
1   teaspoon ground black pepper
¼   cup Parmesan cheese, grated
¼ + ¼ cup bread crumbs
2   tablespoons margarine

Heat oven to 350ºF.
1. Cut cho cho in half (length-wise) and boil in salted water for 20 minutes or until tender.
2. Remove and discard the seed.
3. Using a spoon, carefully remove the flesh from the cho cho halves keeping the skins intact.
    Do not throw out the skins.
4. Mash the flesh using a fork. Set aside.
5. Add ground beef, onion, thyme, scotch bonnet pepper, beef bouillon, and ground black pepper
    to a medium frying pan. Fry until ground beef is well cooked. Drain.
6. Add mashed cho cho, ¼ cup bread crumbs, and Parmesan cheese to ground beef mixture. Mix well.
7. Fill cho cho skins with a heaping amount of the stuffing mixture.
8. Sprinkle the top of the stuffed cho cho with ¼ cup breadcrumbs mixed with 2 tablespoons margarine.
9. Bake in oven until tops are golden brown.
Makes 6 servings.

*See NOTES: Cho cho - Page 72.

TRIPE and BEANS

TRIPE and BEANS

2½ pounds cow tripe, cut in bite-sized pieces
    Vinegar
1 + 1 teaspoon Jamaican curry powder
2   stalks scallion, chopped
½ + ½ teaspoon ground ginger
1   large onion, chopped
3   cloves garlic, chopped
3   teaspoons instant chicken bouillon
1   teaspoon black pepper
2   tablespoons vegetable oil
4   cups water
¼   cup milk
1   medium tomato, chopped
2   (15 ounce) can butter beans, drained
    Salt to taste
    Cornstarch or all-purpose flour

1. Wash tripe with a mixture of vinegar and water. Discard liquid.
2. Season tripe with 1 teaspoon curry powder, scallion, ½ teaspoon ginger, onion, garlic, salt, and black pepper.
3. Marinate in refrigerator overnight, or for at least 1 hour.
4. Heat vegetable oil in pressure cooker*. Add 1 teaspoon curry powder and ½ teaspoon ginger. Cook for about 2 minutes, stirring continuously.
5. Add seasoned tripe and water to pressure cooker*.
6. Cover and seal pressure cooker*. Pressure-cook for about 35 minutes or until tripe is tender.
7. Allow pressure cooker to fully cool before opening.
8. Add milk, tomato, and butter beans. Salt to taste.
9. Thicken with flour or cornstarch, if needed. Simmer for about 10 minutes.

Makes 4 to 6 servings.

*Follow manufacturer's instructions.

SIDE DISHES

Easy Beer

1 lb Self Flour

3 tsp Baking Powder

1 pint Stout (Dragon)

1 Cup Dark Sugar

1 Egg

2 ozs Margarine

Spices – nutmeg, cinnamon, grated
orange peel
vanilla, almond flavouring
Raisins, Prunes chopped – a little
Rum, cherries cut in pieces

Sift flour & baking powder & spices
together. Rub together sugar &
margarine & egg. [illegible]
[illegible]

Copy of Recipe handwritten by Enid Pilliner

BANANA FRITTERS

BANANA FRITTERS

2   ripe bananas, mashed
1   cup all-purpose flour*
1½ teaspoon baking powder
1   egg, beaten
½   teaspoon ground orange peel
½   teaspoon ground nutmeg
1   tablespoon granulated sugar
    Vegetable oil for frying
1   teaspoon cinnamon
¼   cup granulated sugar

1. Add beaten egg, 2 tablespoons granulated sugar, ground orange peel, and nutmeg to mashed bananas.
2. Combine flour* and baking powder. Fold into banana mixture.
3. Heat enough oil to cover bottom of non-stick frying pan.
4. Drop batter by spoonfuls into medium-hot oil. Adjust heat to prevent burning.
5. Fry** until cooked and golden brown on both sides.
6. Drain on absorbent paper.
7. Sprinkle on both sides with granulated sugar and cinnamon mixture.
Serve warm.
Makes 12 to 16 Banana Fritters.

*Self-rising flour may be used, omitting the baking powder and salt.
**Test cook time before adding too many raw fritters to frying pan. Because of the sugar in the bananas, these tend to burn easily.

CABBAGE, CARROT and TOMATO SALAD

CABBAGE, CARROT and TOMATO SALAD

1   small cabbage, finely sliced
2   medium carrots, grated
1   medium tomato, cubed
¼   cup white vinegar
½   teaspoon salt
¼   teaspoon ground black pepper
½   teaspoon granulated sugar

1. Mix together vinegar, salt, black pepper, and granulated sugar. Set aside.
2. Combine cabbage, carrot, and tomato.
3. Stir vinegar mixture. Add to vegetables.
4. Refrigerate for at least 30 minutes before serving.
Makes 4 to 6 servings.

CORN
FRITTERS

CORN FRITTERS

1   (8 ounce) can whole kernel sweet corn, drained
1   cup all-purpose flour*
1½ teaspoons baking powder
1   teaspoon salt
1   egg, beaten
¼   cup milk
1   tablespoon granulated sugar
2   teaspoons melted butter or margarine
    Vegetable oil for frying
1   teaspoon cinnamon
¼   cup granulated sugar

1. Sift and mix flour, baking powder, and salt.
2. Combine beaten egg, milk, granulated sugar, and melted butter.
3. Fold flour into egg mixture.
4. Add corn. Allow batter to sit for about 3 minutes.
5. Heat enough oil to cover the bottom of a non-stick frying pan.
6. Drop batter by spoonfuls into medium-hot oil.
7. Fry until cooked and golden brown on both sides.
8. Drain on absorbent paper.
9. Sprinkle both sides with granulated sugar and cinnamon mixture.
Makes 12 to 16 Corn Fritters.

*Self-rising flour may be used, omitting the baking powder and salt.

CORN
PUDDING

CORN PUDDING

5   eggs, lightly beaten
⅓   cup butter
2   tablespoons granulated sugar
½   cup milk
1   (15 ounce) can whole kernel sweet corn, drained
1   (15 ounce) can cream style corn
¼   teaspoon vanilla extract (optional)
4   tablespoons cornstarch

Heat oven to 390° F.
1. Grease 2-quart casserole dish.
2. Add melted butter, granulated sugar, and milk to eggs.
3. Whisk in cornstarch until smooth.
4. Stir in whole corn, creamed corn, and vanilla.
5. Bake for about 1 hour or until cooked and golden brown.
Makes 6 to 8 servings.

FRIED DUMPLINGS

Fried Dumplings are some times called Johnny Cakes – a corruption of the words 'journey cakes'. They were easy to make and they would not spoil if you were taking a long journey.

FRIED DUMPLINGS
(JOHNNY CAKES)

2   cups all-purpose flour
1   tablespoon granulated sugar
½   teaspoon salt
1½ teaspoons baking powder
1   tablespoon margarine, melted
¼   cup water
¼   cup milk
    Vegetable oil for frying

1. Combine milk and water.
2. Sift and mix flour, granulated sugar, baking powder, and salt.
3. Cut in margarine and add enough milk/water mixture to make a smooth dough.
4. Place dough in a covered container and put to relax for about 30 minutes.
5. Roll dough to ½ inch thickness.
6. Cut rounds with a small cutter.
7. Fry in hot oil until cooked and golden brown on all sides.

Best if served hot, but can be served at room temperature.

Makes 12 to 14 Fried Dumplings.

MACARONI and CHEESE

Macaroni and Cheese was always a dish that was sliced, not spooned.

MACARONI and CHEESE

2	cups elbow macaroni	2	cups milk
2	eggs, beaten	2	teaspoons instant chicken bouillon
3½	cups cheddar cheese, shredded	1	teaspoon dry mustard
3 + 1	tablespoon butter or margarine	½	teaspoon black pepper
1	medium onion, chopped		Salt to taste
¼	cup all-purpose flour	½	cup fresh bread crumbs

Heat oven to 375º F.
1. Prepare macaroni as per instructions on package.
2. Drain macaroni and pour into greased 2-quart casserole dish.
3. Add beaten eggs and 1 cup of shredded cheese to macaroni. Mix to coat macaroni.
4. Saute chopped onion in 3 tablespoon of butter or margarine.
5. Stir in all-purpose flour and cook for 1 minute.
6. Slowly stir in milk, chicken bouillon, mustard, and black pepper.
7. Cook on low heat, stirring until smooth.
8. Add 2 cups of shredded cheese to milk, stir until cheese is melted. Add salt to taste.
9. Pour cheese sauce over macaroni, mixing until sauce is evenly distributed.
10. Top with remaining ½ cup of shredded cheese.
11. Melt 1 tablespoon of butter or margarine. Stir into bread crumbs.
12. Sprinkle over top layer of cheese.
13. Bake uncovered for about 30 minutes.
14. Allow to cool for about 15 to 20 minutes.
Makes 10 to 12 side servings, or 6 main-dish servings.

RICE and PEAS

Sunday lunch or dinner would not be complete without Rice and Peas made with red kidney beans or pigeon peas (called gungo peas in Jamaica).

RICE and PEAS

2   cups dried red kidney beans or pigeon (gungo) peas, soaked in water overnight*

1½ cups coconut milk   Salt to taste

1½ cups water   ½   teaspoon black pepper

1   stalk scallion, chopped   3   slices bacon, diced

1   small onion, diced   2   cups uncooked rice

2   sprigs fresh thyme   1   scotch bonnet pepper, whole

3   teaspoons instant chicken bouillon

1. Boil dried red kidney beans or pigeon peas in 4 cups of water until tender.
2. Retain 1½ cups of the water that the beans were cooked in.
3. To the cooked beans and water, add coconut milk and bring to a boil.
4. Add all remaining ingredients except the rice and scotch bonnet pepper. Cook for about 5 minutes.
5. Stir in rice and the scotch bonnet pepper.
6. Cover and bring to a boil. Reduce heat.
7. Stir** occasionally for the first 10 minutes of cooking.
8. Cook for about 35 minutes, or until rice grains are soft and all liquid absorbed.

*Canned red kidney beans may be used, but the final product will not have the traditional, dark red color that dry beans produce.

**Be careful not to burst the scotch bonnet pepper when stirring.

See NOTES: Scotch Bonnet Pepper - Page 74.

SALT FISH FRITTERS

Homemade salt fish fritters were never as good as those sold by neighborhood vendor, Mother Young. She made the best salt fish fritters – they were always hot and greasy, and the highpoint was actually finding a piece of salt fish!

We later found out that our mother always gave Mother Young extra money to make fritters because she knew that we loved them and always bought from her.

A Tapper Family Memory

SALT FISH* FRITTERS

½ pound boneless salted fish (cod or pollock)	1 egg, beaten
2 cups all-purpose flour	¼ teaspoon black pepper
1 cup milk or water	½ teaspoon dried thyme
1 small onion, chopped	Salt to taste
1 stalk scallion, chopped	Vegetable oil for frying

1. Boil salted fish for about 15 minutes or until tender.
2. Drain and flake salted fish.
3. Combine flour and milk or water and beat to a smooth paste.
4. Beat in egg.
5. Add flaked salted fish, onion, and scallion. Mix well.
6. Season to taste with salt and pepper.
7. Mixture should be a thick batter that falls easily off a spoon.
8. Heat enough oil to cover the bottom of a non-stick frying pan.
9. Drop batter by spoonfuls into medium-hot oil.
10. Fry until cooked and golden brown on both sides.
11. Drain on absorbent paper.

Serve warm.

Makes 18 to 20 Salt Fish Fritters.

*See NOTES: Salt Fish - Page 73.

DESSERTS

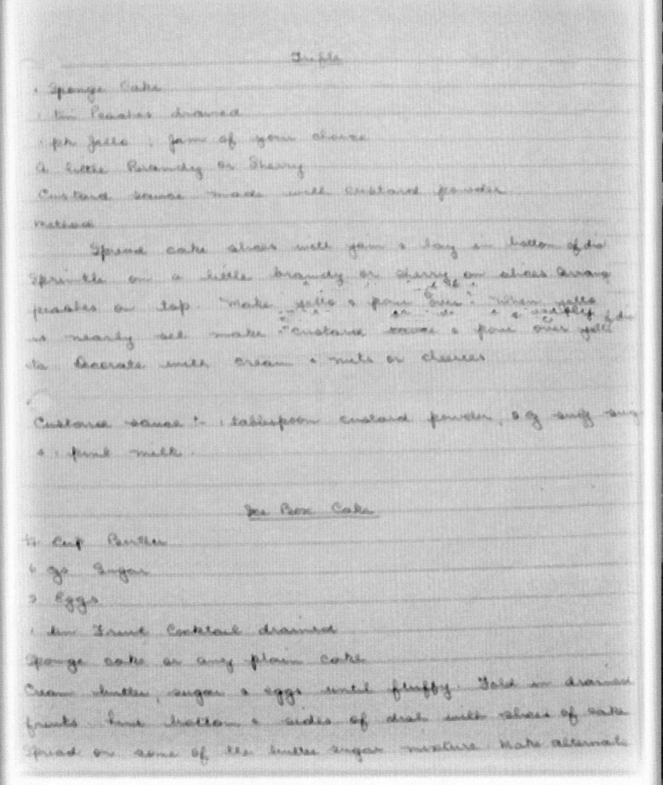

Trifle

Sponge Cake
tin Peaches drained
pkt jelly : jam of your choice
a little Brandy or Sherry
Custard sauce made with custard powder

method

Spread cake slices with jam & lay in bottom of dish
Sprinkle on a little brandy or sherry on slices. Arrange
peaches on top. Make jello & pour over. When jello
is nearly set make custard sauce & pour over jello
etc. Decorate with cream & nuts or cherries

Custard sauce :- 1 tablespoon custard powder, & g suff sugar
& 1 pint milk.

Ice Box Cake

½ cup Butter
6 g Sugar
2 Eggs
1 tin Fruit Cocktail drained
sponge cake or any plain cake

Cream butter, sugar & eggs until fluffy. Fold in drained
fruits. Line bottom & sides of dish with slices of cake
spread on some of the butter sugar mixture. Make alternate

APPLE COFFEE CAKE

Apples that are used to make traditional apple pies were not easily available in Jamaica – we referred to such apples as "American Apples".

Our Mother, who was the consummate and curious cook, made do with making "mock apple" pies using cho cho (chayote squash), or the native Otahiti Apple. One day she got her hands on a can of apple pie filling and on the label was the recipe for a coffee cake. She tried it, we liked it, and it became a family favorite with a few tweaks along the way.

A Pilliner Family Memory

APPLE COFFEE CAKE
WARNING: Nuts are used in this recipe, but are optional

1 (20 ounce) can apple pie filling	1½ cups milk
2 teaspoons cinnamon	½ cup margarine, softened
3 cups all-purpose flour*	3 eggs
3 teaspoons baking powder*	¼ cup packed brown sugar
½ teaspoon salt*	¼ cup coarsely chopped walnuts (optional)
1 cup granulated sugar	2 tablespoons margarine or butter, melted

Heat oven to 350ºF (325ºF if using glass bakeware).
Grease 9 x 9 x 3 inch pan.

1. Mix pie filling and cinnamon. Set aside.
2. Beat all-purpose flour*, baking powder*, salt*, granulated sugar, milk, margarine, and eggs in large bowl on low speed for about 2 minutes, scraping sides of bowl often.
3. Pour half of batter into prepared pan.
4. Spoon half of the pie filling mixture over the batter mixture.
5. Repeat steps with remaining batter and apple mixture.
6. Sprinkle top with mixture of brown sugar, walnuts, and melted margarine.
7. Bake for 45 to 55 minutes, or until knife inserted comes out clean.
8. Optional: Spread glaze topping over cake after it has cooled for approximately 20 minutes.

Glaze Topping: Mix together ¾ cup powdered sugar, 1 tablespoon margarine, ¾ teaspoon vanilla flavoring, and 2 to 3 teaspoons of hot water, until smooth.

*Self-rising flour may be used, omitting baking powder and salt.

BANANA BREAD

BANANA BREAD
WARNING: Nuts are used in this recipe, but are optional.

½ cup butter or margarine
½ cup granulated sugar
1   egg, beaten
1   teaspoon vanilla extract
3   large ripe bananas, mashed
2   cups all-purpose flour
2   teaspoons baking powder
¼   teaspoon baking soda
½   teaspoon salt
¼   teaspoon ground nutmeg
½   cup raisins or chopped walnuts (optional)
½   cup milk (use if needed)

Heat oven to 350ºF (325ºF if using glass bakeware).
Grease 9-inch loaf pan.
1. Cream butter and granulated sugar.
2. Add beaten egg and vanilla.
3. Add mashed bananas into butter mixture.
4. Sift flour, baking powder, baking soda, salt, and nutmeg.
5. Mix dry ingredients into banana mixture.
6. Fold in raisins or walnuts (optional).
7. Mixture should drop easily from a spoon. If necessary, add milk until proper consistency is reached.
8. Pour into greased loaf pan.
9. Bake for 1 hour or until golden brown and a knife inserted comes out clean.
Makes 6 to 8 servings.

BREAD PUDDING

Bread Pudding is a very popular dessert in Jamaica.

Also popular, when we were children, was stewed prunes and evaporated milk.

BREAD PUDDING

8 slices of white bread, lightly toasted	⅓ cup granulated sugar
2 tablespoons butter or margarine	1 teaspoon vanilla flavoring
⅓ cup brown sugar	1 teaspoon almond flavoring
½ teaspoon cinnamon	¼ teaspoon salt
⅓ cup raisins	2½ cups milk, scalded
3 eggs, slightly beaten	⅓ cup strawberry jam (or your favorite), optional

Heat oven to 350ºF.

Grease 1½-quart oven-proof glass dish.

1. Spread butter or margarine on toast.
2. Sprinkle brown sugar and cinnamon on buttered toast.
3. Put two toasted slices together, making 4 sandwiches.
4. Remove crusts, then cut each sandwich into 4 rectangles.
5. Arrange toast in bottom of baking dish.
6. Sprinkle with raisins.
7. Blend eggs, granulated sugar, vanilla flavoring, almond flavoring, and salt.
8. Add egg mixture to milk.
9. Pour milk mixture over layers of toast.
10. Place baking dish in pan of very hot water about 1 inch deep.
11. Bake 60 to 65 minutes, or until knife inserted comes out clean.
12. Remove baking dish from water.
13. Spread strawberry jam over top of Bread Pudding.

Serve warm or cold.

Makes 6 to 9 servings.

CHRISTMAS CAKE

Also called Fruit Cake, Wedding Cake, or Black Cake by Jamaicans. It is not to be confused with the much maligned fruit cake of American cuisine.

CHRISTMAS CAKE

WARNING: This recipe uses red wine and rum which are alcoholic beverages.

3	eggs	½	tablespoon mixed spice (pumpkin spice)
1	cup brown sugar	1	teaspoon almond flavoring
1	cup margarine	1	teaspoon vanilla flavoring
2	cups all-purpose flour	4	teaspoons browning (burnt sugar)
2	teaspoons baking powder	1	cup red wine*
1	cup bread crumbs	2	cups mixed fruits (raisins, prunes, cherries, currants) that have been chopped up and soaked in red wine* and rum*
1	teaspoon nutmeg		

Heat oven to 350ºF.

Grease 10 x 2-inch metal baking pan.

1. Cream brown sugar and margarine until fluffy.
2. Gradually beat in eggs.
3. Combine all-purpose flour, baking powder, bread crumbs, nutmeg, and mixed spices.
4. Add egg mixture to dry ingredients.
5. Add almond flavoring, vanilla flavoring, browning (burnt sugar), red wine, and soaked mixed fruits.
6. Pour batter into greased baking pan.
7. Cover with tin foil and place in a pan of very hot water about 1 inch deep.
8. Bake for 1½ hours, or until a knife inserted comes out clean.

Makes 12 to 14 servings.

Serve with Hard Sauce.

½ cup butter, 1½ cup powdered sugar, and 2 tablespoons rum*.

Cream butter and powdered sugar. Add rum*.

Refrigerate.

*Red wine and rum are alcoholic beverages.

CINNAMON BUNS

CINNAMON BUNS

3 cups all-purpose flour	¼ cup butter or margarine
4 teaspoons baking powder	½ cup raisins
1 teaspoon salt	¼ cup corn syrup
½ cup butter or margarine	2 tablespoons butter or margarine, softened
¾ cup milk	¼ cup brown sugar
¾ cup granulated sugar	2 teaspoons cinnamon
¼ cup brown sugar	

Heat oven to 350º F (325º F, if using glass bakeware).
1. Sift and mix flour, baking powder, and salt in large bowl.
2. Cut in butter or margarine.
3. Add enough milk to make a soft dough.
4. Refrigerate dough for about 1 hour.
5. Boil granulated sugar, brown sugar, and ¼ cup butter or margarine for one minute.
6. Pour into 13 x 9-inch baking pan. Set aside.
7. Combine corn syrup, butter or margarine, brown sugar, cinnamon, and raisins. Set aside.
8. Turn out dough onto lightly floured surface. Roll into rectangle ¼ inch thick.
9. Spread raisin mixture over dough.
10. Roll up dough, jelly-roll style from the long side to the other long side. Cut roll crosswise about 1 to 1¼ inch wide.
11. Place in pan with boiled sugar mixture, cut side down.
12. Bake for about 40 minutes or until golden brown.
13. Remove baking pan from oven and let sit for 5 minutes.
14. Loosen sides with a table knife. Place a platter over baking pan and turn upside down. Leave pan over platter for 5 minutes to allow sugar mixture to drizzle over buns. Remove pan.

Makes 12 to 14 Cinnamon Buns.

TIP: To get perfectly round Cinnamon Buns, you may use medium-sized muffin tins instead of a 13 x 9-inch baking pan.

COCONUT DROPS

COCONUT DROPS

1   dried coconut*, diced and washed
1   cup brown sugar
1½ tablespoons ground ginger

1. Combine coconut, ginger, and brown sugar in a small saucepan.
2. Boil on slow heat, stirring occasionally, until coconut is tender (about 30 minutes).
3. Drop by spoonfuls on cookie tray that has been lined with wax paper.
4. Allow to cool.

Makes 8 to 10 Coconut Drops.

*See NOTES: Dried Coconut - Page 72.

CORNMEAL PUDDING

CORNMEAL PUDDING

1½ cups cornmeal
½   cup all-purpose flour
1   teaspoon salt
1   teaspoon ground nutmeg
½ + ¼ teaspoon ground cinnamon
¾ + ⅛ cup brown sugar
1   teaspoon vanilla flavoring
½   teaspoon almond extract
3 + ½ cups coconut milk
½   cup raisins, coated with flour
¼   butter or margarine, melted

Heat oven to 350ºF (325ºF if using glass bakeware).
Grease 3-quart baking pan.
1. Combine cornmeal, all-purpose flour, salt, nutmeg, and ½ teaspoon cinnamon.
2. Combine ¾ cup brown sugar, vanilla, almond flavoring, and 3 cups coconut milk. Heat in a sauce pan until slightly warm.
3. Add half of liquid to cornmeal mixture. Stir until there are no lumps, then add remaining liquid and mix until smooth.
4. Pour into baking pan.
5. Sprinkle flour-coated raisins into mixture.
6. Bake for 15 minutes. Remove baking pan from oven and thoroughly stir pudding mixture.
7. Combine ½ cup coconut milk, melted butter or margarine, and ⅛ cup brown sugar. Pour on top of stirred pudding. Sprinkle with cinnamon.
8. Return to the oven and bake for 1 hour.
9. Top will still be soft, but will thicken when pudding cools.
Serve warm or at room temperature.
Makes 10 to 14 servings.

EASTER
STOUT BUN

Eating bun with cheese, and flying kites, were traditions at Easter when we were children.

Good Friday service at our church was always 3 hours long and started at Noon. When we were young children, the only thing that made the time bearable, was the bun and cheese that Mother brought to keep us satisfied, and the sound of the town clock chiming on the half-hour and hour.

A Pilliner Family Memory

EASTER STOUT* BUN
WARNING: This recipe uses stout which is an alcoholic beverage

3 cups all-purpose flour	3 tablespoons butter or margarine
3 teaspoons bakting powder	1 tablespoon browning (burnt sugar)
½ teaspoon ground nutmeg	1 teaspoon vanilla flavoring
½ teaspoon ground cinnamon	½ cup maraschino cherries, chopped
2 cups stout (Dragon® or Guinness®)*	½ cup raisins
1 cup brown sugar	¼ cup honey
1 egg, beaten	

Heat oven to 350ºF.

Grease a 9-inch loaf pan.

1. Mix and sift flour, baking powder, and spices.
2. Heat stout, browning (burnt sugar), margarine, brown sugar, vanilla flavoring, and eggs in a small saucepan.
3. Add stout mixture to dry ingredients.
4. Fold in cherries and raisins.
5. Pour into baking pan.
6. Bake for 40 to 45 minutes, or until knife inserted comes out clean.
7. Allow to cool, then brush top of Easter Bun with honey.

Serve at room temperature with cheese and/or butter.

*Stout is an alcoholic beverage.

EGG CUSTARD

Egg Custard was always paired with flavored gelatin dessert.

When we were children, the only brand that was available was Shirriff' Lushus® Jelly Gelatin Dessert with its "Flavoured Bud" that melted when hot water was added to it.

EGG CUSTARD

8   egg yolks, beaten
2   cups milk or 1 can evaporated milk
1   cup granulated sugar
2   teaspoons vanilla flavoring
¼ + ¼ teaspoon nutmeg

Heat oven to 325ºF.
1. Combine all ingredients and pour into 1½-quart baking dish or individual ramekins.
2. Place dish(es) in a pan with ½ to 1 inch of hot water.
3. Bake for about 25 minutes, or until knife inserted comes out clean.
4. Remove from oven and sprinkle with nutmeg.
Makes 6 servings.

Optional: After removing custard from oven, top with a glaze made from ¼ teaspoon granulated sugar mixed with ⅛ cup of water.

GIZZADS

GIZZADS

Pastry dough (enough for a 9-inch pie)
1 cup water
1 cup brown sugar*
½ teaspoon ground nutmeg
½ teaspoon almond flavoring
1½ cups dried coconut*, finely grated**
2 tablespoons butter or margarine
Raisins

Heat oven to 350ºF.
1. Roll out pastry dough to a thin layer.
2. Cut into 4-inch circles. Form a casing by pinching edges for a decorative look.
3. Bake pastry casings for about 10 minutes or until light golden brown.
4. In a medium saucepan, boil water and brown sugar to make a syrup.
5. Add ground nutmeg, almond flavoring, and grated coconut.
6. Boil for about 15 minutes, stirring constantly.
7. Stir in butter or margarine. Allow to cool.
8. Add cooled coconut filling to cooled pastry casings.
9. Decorate each Gizzada with 1 raisin.
10. Return to oven and bake for about 10 minutes or until coconut begins to brown.
Makes 6 - 8 Gizzadas.

*See NOTES: Dried Coconut - Page 72.
**If you use sweetened coconut flakes sold in the baking aisle of a supermarket, you should use less sugar and process the coconut in a blender to make the flakes finer.

GRATER CAKES

GRATER CAKES

3   cups dried coconut*, peeled and grated**
2   cups granulated sugar*
¼   cup water
½   teaspoon almond flavoring
¼   teaspoon salt
     Red food coloring

1. In a mediutm saucepan, boil water and granulated sugar to make a syrup.
2. Add almond flavoring, salt, and grated coconut.
3. Cook until mixture thickens, stirring constantly.
4. Remove ⅓ of coconut mixture and add enough red food coloring to give it a light pink color.
5. Pour remaining coconut mixture into a 1-inch deep greased rectangular pan. Spread evenly.
6. Spread the pink colored coconut mixture over the first layer of coconut.
7. Allow to cool for about 35 to 40 minutes.
8. Cut into 1 to 2 inch pieces.

Makes 6 to 8 Grater Cakes.

*See NOTES: Dried Coconut - Page 72.
**If you use sweetened coconut flakes sold in the baking aisle of a supermarket, you should use less sugar and process the coconut in a blender to make the flakes thinner.

ICE BOX CAKE

This was a favorite in both our families.

Thinking back, we are now surprised (and very grateful), that although raw eggs were always used for this recipe, no one was ever adversely affected.

Don't miss out on experiencing this wonderful dessert; however, we strongly recommend that you use liquid pasteurized eggs.

ICE BOX CAKE
WARNING: Nuts and raw eggs are used in this recipe.
For safety, it is strongly recommended that you use liquid pasteurized eggs as a substitute.

¼ cup butter or margarine, softened
½ cup granulated sugar
2 eggs*, beaten
1 (15 ounce) can fruit cocktail, drained
   Slices of already baked pound cake or yellow cake
   Whipped cream
   Walnut pieces, for decoration (optional)

1. Cream butter, granulated sugar, and eggs until fluffy.
2. Fold in drained fruits.
3. Line bottom and sides of 1-quart rectangular dish with cake slices.
4. Spread butter mixture on layer of cake slices.
5. Add another layer of cake slices, then butter mixture.
6. Decorate top with whipped cream and walnut pieces.
7. Refrigerate for at least 4 hours before cutting.
8. Keep refrigerated until ready to eat.
Makes 6 to 8 servings.

*Substitute ⅓ cup pasteurized liquid eggs.

NO-HOLE DOUGHNUTS

We didn't mind rainy days, because Mother would make these to cheer us up. She didn't have a doughnut cutter, so we only got doughnut holes (really big doughnut holes!).

A Pilliner Family Memory

NO-HOLE DOUGHNUTS

3½ cups all-purpose flour
4 teaspoons baking powder
½ teaspoon salt
¼ teaspoon ground nutmeg
½ teaspoon ground cinnamon
1 teaspoon baking soda

2 eggs, beaten
¾ cup granulated sugar
½ teaspoon vanilla flavoring
1 cup milk
2 tablespoons butter or margarine, melted
Vegetable oil for frying

1. Sift together all-purpose flour, baking powder, salt, nutmeg, cinnamon, and baking soda.
2. Add granulated sugar and vanilla flavoring to eggs. Beat well for about two minutes.
3. Pour milk and butter into egg mixture.
4. Add milk mixture to flour mixture.
5. Stir with fork until dough is smooth.
6. Chill dough for about two hours.
7. Roll out dough on floured surface to approximately ¼ inch thickness. (If necessary, add a small amount of flour to dough.)
8. Cut into circles, or whatever shape you wish.
9. Fry in medium-hot oil until cooked and golden brown. (Adjust heat to prevent burning.)
10. Drain on absorbent paper.
11. Toss cooked No-hole Doughnuts in granulated or powdered sugar and cinnamon.
Serve warm.
Makes approximately 3 dozen No-hole Doughnuts.

PLANTAIN TARTS

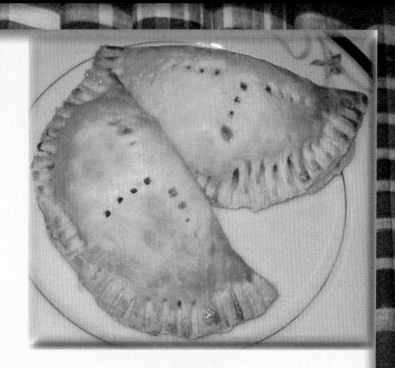

PLANTAIN TARTS

3   large very ripe plantains*
½   teaspoon salt
¼ + ¼ cup granulated sugar
½   teaspoon nutmeg
¼   teaspoon vanilla flavoring

¼   cup raisins (optional)
2   drops red food coloring (traditional, but optional)
    Pastry dough for a two-crust 9-inch pie
1   egg, beaten
    Water

Heat oven to 350°F
1. Peel plantains and cut into 3-inch pieces.
2. Add salt to water and boil plantains for about 30 minutes or until soft. Drain.
3. Mash drained plantain until mixture is smooth.
4. Stir in ¼ cup granulated sugar, nutmeg, vanilla, (raisins and red food coloring, if used).
    If mixture is too stiff, add a small amount of milk.
5. Roll out pastry dough, then cut into circles about 4 inches in diameter.
6. Portion plantain mixture on one side of dough circle, leaving a ½ inch border.
7. Fold the other half of the circle over filling to form a crescent shape.
8. Crimp the edges with a fork to seal.
9. Use a fork to prick small openings in the top of each tart.
10. Brush with beaten egg.
11. Bake on un-greased baking sheet for 25 to 30 minutes or until golden brown.
12. Mix a small amount of water with half of the remaining granulated sugar. Brush onto baked tarts.
13. Optional: Sprinkle with granulated sugar. Cool on wire racks.
Serve warm or at room temperature.
Makes 12 to 14 Plantain Tarts.

*See NOTES: Plantain - Page 73.

ROCK CAKES

Rock Cakes were always available for snacking, or for surprise visitors.

If it was four o'clock on any given day, it was tea time at our house. However, tea time on Sundays was quite a production. The tea trolley would be rolled out to the verandah loaded with delicious treats: buttered toast-fingers dusted with cinnamon and sugar; rock cakes; dainty sandwiches made with colored cheese, cucumber, chicken, or roast beef; and, of course, cake.

A Pilliner Family Memory

ROCK CAKES

2 cups all-purpose flour	½ cup margarine
2 teaspoons baking powder	½ cup raisins
½ + ⅓ cup granulated sugar	1 egg, beaten
½ teaspoon nutmeg	½ cup milk
½ teaspoon ground orange peel	

Heat oven to 350°F.

Grease cookie tray.

1. Combine all-purpose flour, baking powder, granulated sugar, nutmeg, and orange peel in a medium sized bowl.
2. Add margarine to flour mixture and use a dough blender or finger tips to process until mixture resembles fine breadcrumbs.
3. Add raisins.
4. Blend beaten egg and milk.
5. Add to flour mixture and combine using a fork. Do not over mix.
6. Drop by spoonfuls onto greased cookie tray.
7. Bake for about 25 minutes or until golden brown.
8. Remove from oven and sprinkle with remaining sugar.

Cool on wire rack.

Serve at room temperature.

Makes 10 to 12 rock cakes.

SWEET POTATO PUDDING

SWEET POTATO* PUDDING

2 pounds sweet potatoes*, peeled and grated**	
1 cup brown sugar	4 cups coconut milk
½ cup all-purpose flour	3 teaspoons vanilla flavoring
2 teaspoons ground nutmeg	1 cup raisins, coated with flour
2 teaspoons ground mixed spice (pumpkin pie spice)	
1 teaspoon salt	Butter or margarine

Heat oven to 375ºF (350ºF if using glass bake ware).

Grease 10 x 3-inch metal pan.

1. In large bowl, combine all dry ingredients (except raisins).
2. Add coconut milk, vanilla, and grated sweet potatoes.
3. Mix well. Mixture will not be very thick.
4. Pour into baking pan.
5. Sprinkle flour-coated raisins into mixture.
6. Dot generously with butter or margarine.
7. Bake for about 1½ hours or until pudding is set and starts to shrink away from the side of the baking pan.
8. Let set for 30 minutes before cutting into slices.

Serve warm or at room temperature.

Makes 6 to 8 servings.

*Sweet Potato – see NOTES: Sweet Potato - Page 74.

** If you use a blender to grate the potatoes, use some of the coconut milk in this step.

TRIFLE

TRIFLE
WARNING: Contains alcohol and nuts, but use is optional.

4 - 5 slices of already baked pound cake or yellow cake
1   (15 ounce) can sliced peaches, drained
1   (.3 ounce) box of gelatin dessert (strawberry or raspberry)
¼   cup sherry*
    Jam of your choice
    Custard sauce made with Bird's Custard**
    Whipped cream, glazed cherries, and walnut pieces or almond slivers (optional)

1. Spread jam on cake slices.
2. Place a layer of cake slices in a 1½ quart glass bowl.
3. Sprinkle cake with sherry* until cake is moist.
4. Arrange peach slices on top of cake.
5. Prepare gelatin dessert as per instructions on package. Refrigerate until slightly thickened.
6. Pour thickened gelatin dessert over layer of peaches and cake.
7. Refrigerate until gelatin dessert is almost completely set.
8. Prepare Bird's Custard sauce as per instructions on package and allow to cool.
9. Pour custard sauce over layer of gelatin dessert.
10. Decorate with whipped cream, cherries, and chopped walnuts or almond slivers.
11. Refrigerate for at least 6 hours (preferably overnight) before serving.

*Instead of sherry, you may use the juice that was drained from the can of peaches to moisten the cake.

**Substitute for Bird's Custard sauce.
1 egg yolk, beaten; 2 tablespoons granulated sugar; 1 teaspoon vanilla extract; 3 teaspoons cornstarch; 1 cup milk. Combine egg, granulated sugar, and vanilla. Add cornstarch to ½ cup milk and mix until smooth, then add remaining milk. Pour mixtures into saucepan and slowly cook until thickened, stirring constantly. Allow to cool.

...t Chutney. String Raisins blanched
...ngo strips
...ak for 20 - 25 mins

Pumpkin Pone

...ups Pumpkin
" Cornmeal
...gar, spices

...ups Coconut grated
...isins
...juice from Coconut — 3 Cups
... all together. Bake

Cookies

... Vanilla, Nuts
...g's Marg
...lb 2. Sugar
...lb flour

...x all ingredients together & roll into c...
...ke & roll into Icing sugar while hot.

Copy of Recipes handwritten by Enid Pilliner

CHOCOLATE TEA
(HOT CHOCOLATE)

Old-time Jamaicans always referred to any hot drink as "tea". So, there is coffee tea, fish tea (soup), and chocolate tea (hot chocolate).

Jamaican cocoa is renowned and exported worldwide. Almost every family in the countryside had one or two cocoa trees in their yard for their personal use.

The fruit/pod of the cocoa (cacao) tree is oblong-shaped and contains 30 to 50 seeds which are dried, roasted and shelled, then pounded into a paste which is rolled into a medium-sized ball, ready to make Chocolate Tea.

Dunk water crackers in your Chocolate Tea – you'll think you are in heaven!

CHOCOLATE TEA

1   cup prepared chocolate, grated
4   cups water
½   teaspoon grated nutmeg
1   cinnamon stick
     Pinch of salt
     Condensed milk or granulated sugar* to taste
⅓   cup milk*, if needed

1. Bring water to a boil in a medium saucepan.
2. Add grated chocolate, salt, cinnamon stick, and grated nutmeg.
3. Lower heat and simmer for 30 minutes.
4. Remove cinnamon stick and strain chocolate mixture.
5. Sweeten with condensed milk or granulated sugar*.

*If using granulated sugar as sweetener, add ⅓ cup milk to mixture.

EGG and STOUT PUNCH

Drinking this punch was a Christmas morning tradition.

We would drink this after returning home from early-morning church service, and just before having a delicious breakfast of ham and eggs.

A Pilliner Family Memory

EGG and STOUT* PUNCH
WARNING: Alcohol and raw eggs are used in this recipe.
For safety, it is strongly recommended that you use liquid pasteurized eggs as a substitute.

3 medium eggs**, beaten
½ cup granulated sugar
1½ cups evaporated milk
1 cup stout* (Dragon® or Guinness®)
1 teaspoon ground nutmeg
1 tablespoon vanilla extract

1. Add granulated sugar, evaporated milk, stout, nutmeg, and vanilla to beaten eggs.
2. Blend for about 1 minute or until sugar is dissolved.
3. Serve over crushed ice.
Makes 6 to 8 servings.

*Stout is an alcoholic beverage.
**¾ to 1 cup of pasteurized liquid eggs.

GINGER BEER
This is NOT an alcoholic beverage.

GINGER BEER*

1 pound fresh ginger root, washed and finely chopped

8 + 2 cups water

2 cups granulated sugar

1 teaspoon vanilla flavoring

½ cup lime juice

1. Bring chopped ginger and 8 cups water to a boil. Turn off heat.
2. Let cool – cooling may take several hours. Ginger flavor will be more concentrated if you allow the mixture to cool overnight.
3. Strain ginger mixture.
4. Mix granulated sugar with 2 cups water. Bring to a boil to form a syrup. Turn off heat. Let cool.
5. Add cooled syrup, lime juice, and vanilla to strained ginger mixture.
6. Test for sweetness and flavor** and adjust to your taste.
7. Keep refrigerated.

*This is not an alcoholic beverage.
**This recipe will produce a very strong ginger taste. More water and ice may be added for a milder flavor.

PIMENTO DRAM
(A LIQUEUR)

When we were growing up, a liquor cart was always prominently displayed in Jamaican houses. Pimento Dram is a liqueur which would be on such a liquor cart.

Pimento Dram was relatively easy and inexpensive to make – the Pimento tree was everywhere.

PIMENTO DRAM (LIQUEUR)
WARNING: This is an alcoholic beverage.

¼ cup whole pimento (allspice)* seeds
1   cup red rum**   1¼ cups water
1   cinnamon stick   1   cup brown sugar

1. Crush or grind the pimento (allspice) seeds. This should be coarse, large pieces and not a fine grind.
2. Place the crushed pimento (allspice) in a glass jar that can be sealed.
3. Add the rum*, seal the jar, and shake well.
4. Allow this mixture to steep for 4 days. Shake daily.
5. On day 5, break up the cinnamon stick and add it to the mixture.
6. After 12 days total steeping, strain out the solids through a fine-mesh strainer. Then strain again through a coffee filter into final container.
7. Heat water and brown sugar on medium heat, stirring to dissolve the brown sugar. Boil for about 5 minutes. Let the syrup cool.
8 Add syrup to the strained pimento (allspice) mixture.
9. Shake and then let rest for a minimum of two days before using.

*See NOTES: Pimento (Allspice) - Page 73.
** Rum is an alcoholic beverage. You may use more rum to suit your taste.

RUM PUNCH

This verse has always been used as a memory tool for Jamaican Rum Punch recipe:

1 of Sour,

2 of Sweet,

3 of Strong,

and

4 of Weak

RUM* PUNCH
WARNING: This is an alcoholic beverage.

1   cup lime juice (1 of sour)
2   cups fruit (cherry or strawberry) syrup (2 of sweet)
3   cups rum* (3 of strong)
4   cups water or fruit juice** (4 of weak)

1. Mix all ingredients together. Serve over ice.

*For the traditional Rum Punch, which is very strong, Jamaican 100% over proof white rum is used. For a milder version, use a red rum.

*Rum is an alcoholic beverage.

**Fruit juice can be substituted for water which will give the punch a more flavorful taste.

SORREL DRINK

The Sorrel plant is a member of the Hibiscus family. It has a tangy taste and is high in Vitamin C.

Because Sorrel petals are harvested in December, drinking the dark red drink which it produces, is a tradition during the Christmas season in Jamaica. However, dry Sorrel petals are now available year-round, which means that you can have that Christmas feeling throughout the year.

A popular adult beverage is Sorrel with rum.

SORREL DRINK
WARNING: This will be an alcoholic beverage if rum is added.

1   package of dry sorrel
    Ginger, 5 to 6 one-inch slices
10 whole cloves
9   cups water
1   pound brown sugar
½   cup rum*(optional)

1. Fill large pot with 8 cups of water and bring to a boil.
2. Add ginger, sorrel, and cloves.
3. Boil for 30 minutes.
4. Cover tightly and steep overnight. Strain.
5. Boil 1 cup water and brown sugar until it is dissolved and forms a syrup.
6. Add brown sugar syrup to sorrel liquid.
7. Optional: add rum to taste.
Serve over ice.

*Rum is an alcoholic beverage.

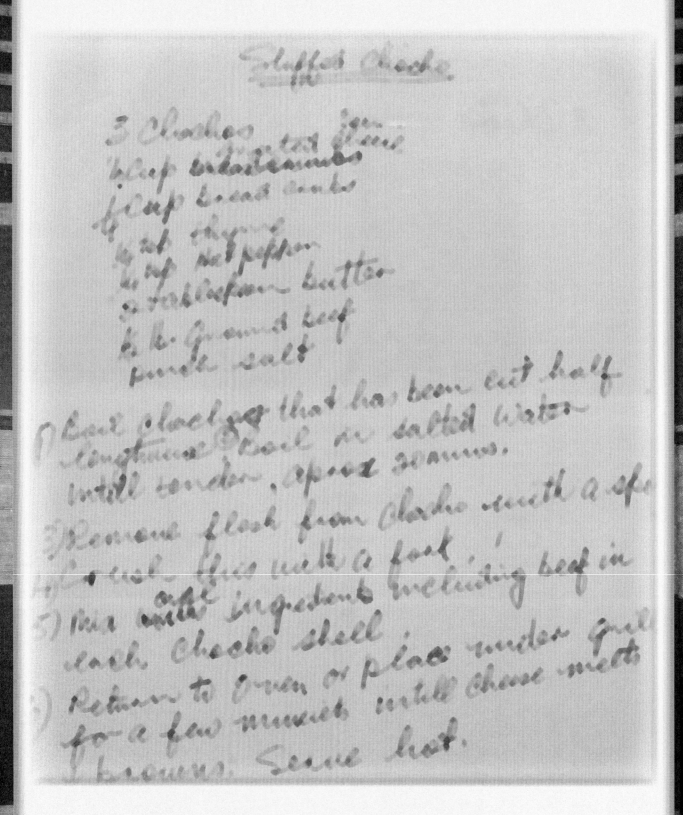

Stuffed Chocho

3 Chochos
½ cup water chive
½ cup bread crumbs
¼ tsp. thyme
¼ tsp. hot pepper
2 tablespoon butter
½ lb. Ground beef
pinch salt

1) Boil chochos that has been cut half lengthwise. Boil in salted water until tender, apout 30 mins.

2) Remove flesh from Chocho with a spoon.

3) Crush flesh with a fork.

4) Mix with ingredients including beef in each Chocho shell.

5) Return to oven or place under grill for a few minutes until cheese melts browns. Serve hot.

Copy of Recipe handwritten by Enid Tapper

JERK SEASONING
(For Pork, Chicken, or Fish)

JERK PORK

JERK CHICKEN

JERK SEASONING
(For Pork, Chicken, or Fish)

¼ cup pimento* (allspice) seeds, finely ground
6   stalks scallions, finely chopped
2 or 3 scotch bonnet peppers, chopped (no seeds)
3   cloves garlic, minced
5   bay leaves, crushed
½   tablespoon salt
½   tablespoon ground black pepper
2   tablespoons soy sauce
1   tablespoon vegetable oil

Combine all ingredients and process until it becomes a paste.
Makes about 1 cup seasoning.

1. Rub Jerk Seasoning on chicken, pork, or fish**. Use 1 to 2 tablespoon per pound of chicken, pork, or fish**.
2. Roast until meat is cooked. You may pre-cook meat in the oven, then finish cooking on the grill.

*Pimento (Allspice). See NOTES: Pimento (Allspice) - Page 73.
**Use less seasoning on fish. Wrap fish in aluminum foil, then bake in the oven or on the grill.

SOLOMON GUNDY

Solomon Gundy is a corrupted spelling of Solomon Grundy, a character in a famous European nursery rhyme written by James Orchard Haliwell in 1842.

Any connection to the food spread is not known, but the rhyme was very popular when we were children in Jamaica.

Solomon Grundy,
Born on a Monday,
Christened on Tuesday,
Married on Wednesday,
Took ill on Thursday,
Grew worse on Friday,
Died on Saturday,
Buried on Sunday.
That was the end,
Of Solomon Grundy.

SOLOMON GUNDY

1½ pounds smoked red herring
2   small onions, chopped
2   stalks scallion, chopped
1   teaspoon dried thyme
¾   cup white vinegar
9   pimento (allspice) seeds
2   tablespoons granulated sugar
1   scotch bonnet pepper, chopped (no seeds)
4   tablespoons vegetable oil

1. Soak smoked red herring for 10 minutes.
2. Remove bones and shred into small pieces.
3. Puree chopped onions, scallion, and thyme.
4. Heat white vinegar, pimento (allspice) seeds, and granulated sugar in a medium saucepan on low fire – do not boil.
5. Add red herring to vinegar mixture and cook for 10 minutes.
6. Remove from heat and discard pimento seeds.
7. Add pureed onion mixture, chopped scotch bonnet pepper, and vegetable oil to red herring. Blend for 1 minute.

Keep refrigerated. Shelf-life 14 days.
Makes an excellent appetizer. Serve on crackers.
Optional: Mix in 1 tablespoon sour cream just before using.

NOTES

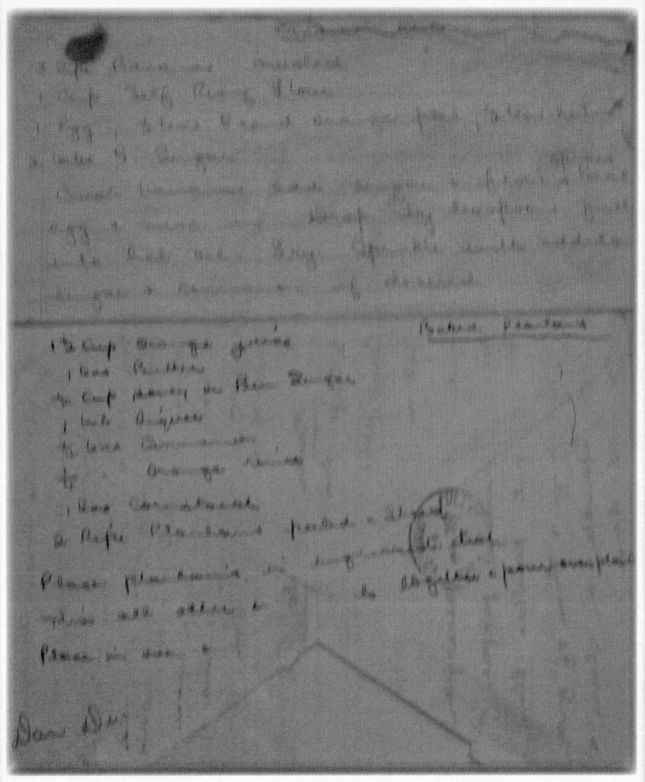

Copy of Recipes handwritten by Enid Pilliner who recorded recipes on any and all forms of writing surfaces. The second of the two recipes shown above was written on a used envelope.

THE ORIGINS
OF JAMAICAN CUISINE

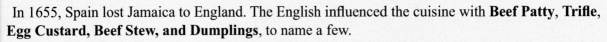

Jamaica's national motto is "Out of Many, One People". This motto not only describes the make-up of the population, but also the Jamaican cuisine. From the time Jamaica was discovered, the people who arrived on the island brought with them the cooking techniques, flavors, spices, and recipes of their homeland. This has resulted in a very flavorful and diverse cuisine.

The native Jamaicans were Arawak Indians who gifted the Jamaican cuisine with cassava and the **bammy**. Unfortunately, the Arawaks were eradicated by disease a few years after the arrival of Europeans.

The first Europeans on the island were the Spanish. Christopher Columbus discovered Jamaica in 1494 on his second voyage to the new world. The Spanish contributed several dishes to the cuisine, most notable of which is the very popular Escoveitch Fish.

In 1655, Spain lost Jamaica to England. The English influenced the cuisine with **Beef Patty**, **Trifle**, **Egg Custard, Beef Stew, and Dumplings**, to name a few.

African slaves were brought to the island to work in the sugar cane fields and the factories where the sugar cane was processed to make molasses, then sugar and rum. With their arrival came the use of root crops (**yellow yam** and **sweet potatoes**), **coconuts, ackees**, dried beans (**Stew Peas** and **Red Peas Soup**), and **bananas**. The **breadfruit**, which was brought from Tahiti in the 18th century by Captain Bligh, was also a cheap source of food for the enslaved workforce.

Slavery was abolished in Jamaica in the 1830's, but sugar and rum had become very lucrative for England, and a 'cheap' labor force was still needed. Indentured workers from India and China were brought to the island, and they brought curry powder, hard-dough bread, and rice. The flavor of Jamaican curry powder is different from the typical Indian curry powder and one reason for this is because it contains pimento (allspice). **Curry Goat** and rice is an island favorite, and curry is also used to flavor chicken (**Curry Chicken**), beef, and seafood (**Curried Dried Shrimp**).

Jamaica gained its independence from England on August 6th, 1962.

COVER PHOTOGRAPH

The background used in the Cover photograph is a madras bandana fabric that is used to make the Jamaica National Costume worn mainly during Festivals and Independence celebrations.

ACKEE

Ackee was brought to Jamaica from West Africa in the 17th century. It is the National Fruit of Jamaica. Ackee and Salt Fish is the National Dish.

Canned Ackee is one of Jamaica's major export products.

BAMMY

Bammy is made from cassava which is a root crop. (Cassava is called yuca and manioc in other parts of the world).

After fresh cassava is grated, the moisture is removed, salt is added, and the mixture is formed into round cakes about ¼ inch thick and 3 to 6 inches in diameter. These cakes are then baked and called Bammy. Before they are eaten, the cakes are soaked in milk and fried until golden brown on both sides.

Bammy can be served at any meal. **Escoveitch Fish** and Bammy is a popular food pairing.

Jamaica exports Bammies to North America and Europe.

BANANAS

Bananas are a staple in the Jamaican diet. Boiled green bananas can be served as an accompaniment to breakfast, lunch, or dinner; and are also used in soups and porridges. Ripe bananas are used in **Banana Bread** and the popular **Banana Fritters**.

Bananas are a major export product from Jamaica to Europe. The 1950's Jamaican Folk Song, The Banana Boat Song (Day-O!), is a work song about loading a ship bound for England with bananas.

BREADFRUIT

Breadfruit is a staple in the Jamaican diet. It can be boiled, roasted, or fried.

CALLALOO

Callaloo is a dark green, leafy vegetable that was brought to Jamaica from West Africa. It is sometimes called Jamaican Spinach and can be steamed or sauteed, and served by itself or combined with salt fish.

CHO CHO

Cho cho is also known as chayote squash, christophene, and chokos in other parts of the world. It has a very bland flavor and is used in stews and soups, or eaten by itself.

Jamaicans have always believed that eating cho cho helps to lower high blood pressure.

DRIED COCONUT
and COCONUT MILK

A mature coconut is referred to as a dried coconut. There is still coconut water in the nut but the flesh is hard. When it is removed from the shell, it can be grated and shredded, and used in cooking.

Coconut milk is the liquid that is obtained when the combination of water and grated dried coconut is squeezed and strained.

Canned coconut milk is widely available.

DUMPLINGS
For Soup And Stew

Mix 1 cup all-purpose flour and a pinch of salt with ½ cup water to make a dough. Cut off small pieces of dough and roll between your hands to make what is called a "spinner" about 2 inches long. Allow to rest for 5 to 10 minutes.

1 cup all-purpose flour will make about 12 spinners.

PIMENTO (ALLSPICE)

Jamaican Pimento (Allspice) should not be confused with the small, sweet, red pepper that is also called pimento or pimiento, and is usually found stuffed in olives.

Dried Pimento berries are widely used in Jamaican cooking. It is used in the world-famous **Jerk Seasoning, Stew Peas,** and **Escoveitch Fish** to name a few.

Pimento is also known as Allspice. This word was coined in the 17th century by English explorers who thought Pimento had the flavors of cinnamon, nutmeg, and cloves.

PLANTAIN

Plantain is a favorite in the Jamaican diet. They can be eaten green (fried), and ripe (fried, boiled, baked). When the plantain ripens it changes from green to yellow to black, and becomes sweeter and softer.

PUMPKIN

This is not the North American pumpkin that is used in pies at Thanksgiving and carved at Halloween. This is the West Indian pumpkin which is also known as Calabaza squash. Butternut squash or Seminole squash may be used as a substitute.

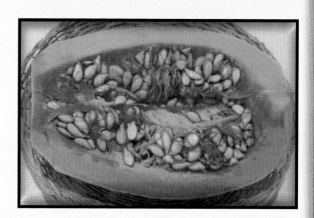

SALT FISH

Salt Fish (Salted Fish: Cod or Pollock) has been a staple of Jamaican cuisine since the 16th century when Canadians brought it to the Caribbean and used it to barter for molasses, rum, and sugar. Salt fish is called bacalao in Latin America.

A bone-less and moist variety is now available; but a few years ago, before cooking salt fish it was necessary to rehydrate it by soaking it overnight, and then removing the many bones.

Salt fish is used in the Jamaican National Dish, **Ackee and Salt Fish.**

SCOTCH BONNET PEPPER

The Scotch Bonnet Pepper is widely used in Jamaican cooking. It is named for its resemblance to the shape of a Scottish Bonnet (Tam o' Shanter). They change from green to yellow, orange or red when ripe.

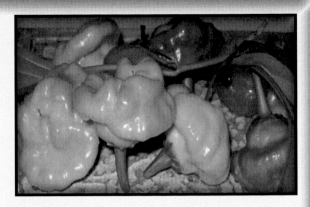

This species of hot pepper is closely related to the Mexican Habanero; but the Scotch Bonnet is hotter and much more flavorful. The seeds are where the Scotch Bonnet is hottest. It is recommended that you remove the seeds before you use the Scotch Bonnet pepper.

TIP: When a recipe calls for the use of a whole scotch bonnet pepper, it is recommended that you loosely wrap the pepper in a small piece of aluminum foil, leaving the top of the package open until the final minutes of cooking. This will ensure that the pepper does not burst.

SWEET POTATO

The Sweet Potato used in Jamaican recipes is light-yellow inside. These recipes are NOT for the sweet potatoes that are also know as Yams in the USA, and are orange inside.

YELLOW YAM

Yam is a starchy tuber, which is a food staple in the Caribbean, Latin America, and some countries in Africa and Asia. It is called namé in Latin America.

There are several varieties of yam, such as White Yam, but Yellow Yam is the most versatile of the yams found in Jamaica. It can be roasted, boiled, or fried. It is an essential ingredient in Jamaican soups.

IN LOVING MEMORY

Enid Pilliner   **&**   ***Enid Tapper***

Sadly, neither of our mothers has cooked for us in a long time. Enid Pilliner passed away in 2005, after a long battle with Alzheimers; and, as fate would have it, Enid Tapper is currently battling the same life-altering disease.

We continued our mothers' tradition by caring for our families and putting them first, just the way we lived and learned. And, our families are also doing the same – caring for their families in the Pilliner and Tapper way with love, devotion, and good food!

Trudy, Maureen, **and** ***Rebecca***

Made in the USA
Middletown, DE
14 August 2017